PARADE

PARADE

A SWIMMING WITH
ELEPHANTS ANTHOLOGY

About Swimming with Elephants Publications, LLC

Why Swimming with Elephants? is a question I am regularly asked. Why that name? That image? What does it reference? Where does it come from?

Picture the Indian Ocean: crystal clear except for the reflection of sky in vibrant blue. See the beast: dusty gray, larger than life, she creeps from land into warm waters. Wading further into the blue until her feet no longer touch the pale sand of the ocean floor. Watch as she lifts her massive legs into a paddle, floating her body, moving gracefully through the silk of a placid sea. This incredibly large, thick skinned creature, heavy and slow moving, is suddenly softened and weightless as she peddles through the water. Something gigantic creating a simple ripple, a tiny wake, a small disturbance of the universe.

If I were an artist, I would paint it. If I was a photographer I would hold a pose until I caught the most perfect picture. But I am a writer, so I attempt to create the image with words and hold it on page. I named the publishing company Swimming with Elephants Publications as a metaphor for being able to exist alongside something magnificent.

Ever since I was a little girl, I always wanted to run my own poetry magazine. I think I wanted it even more than seeing my own work in print. I wanted to create a community of writers who worked together, supported each other, and found an audience for their words. That is where the foundation for Swimming with Elephants Publications, LLC was formed. With this small press, I am attempting to create a community of writers where there is room for different styles, different philosophies, and different objectives, but the overall model is supportive and encouraging.

By 2013, I had some successes with my own writing: two full-length collections of poetry, two chapbooks, and multiple publications in poetry magazines and ezines. These various publications were extremely encouraging to my goals to become a writer, but I wanted to do more than just write. I wanted a community. As I pursued my craft as a writer, I was also observant to the publishing process and the promotional aspect of writing. I noticed how my work was handled when it was accepted for publication as well as when it was rejected. I noticed how magazines and small presses promoted themselves, their authors, and how their products ended up in the hands of readers. I catalogued all the things that helped me as a writer, hurt me as a writer, and made me indifferent.

I served on the editorial staff for several poetry magazines, ezines, and journals, and for several years was an annual judge for a poetry competition run through a now retired website. For over ten years, I taught poetry workshops, participated in poetry performance events, coached a youth slam team, and ran a monthly poetry reading and slam which supported freedom of speech and encouraged the youth. All these experiences directed me to the conclusion: I can help people with their writing. I can help people be heard. I can give people something they need. Hence the elephant was set afloat.

My initial goal was to provide a product for hard working, hustling poets who had powerful and important words to share with an audience eager to listen. I wanted to create a quality product that could be sold at performances so that an audience could take home a little bit of the magic of that performance with them and poets could make a few bucks to help them continue poet-ing. Most importantly, I wanted to take away the power of the press and put the control back in the hands of the writers. After all, it's their words and their product. Basically, I sought to create a small press that, as a writer, I would want to represent me.

What began as a few chapbooks, grew into full length collections, translations, and anthologies.

Today Swimming with Elephants Publications, LLC has more than 50 titles in our line up from poets all over the world. As our parade grew, so did my skills as an editor, book designer, and cover creator. Our process is more stable, and our products are of a higher quality.

We aren't finished yet. We continue to work toward making a better product, increasing distribution, growing our audience, and promoting our poets. We have five years under our belts and are looking forward to the next five.

There are many ways to support our authors: Purchase books from our poets, review books on websites and in print journals, see our poets perform when they come to a town near you, interact with our website and Facebook page, or send them compliments and applause. Supporting our writers and events also helps support our press, but as a not for profit, growth can be difficult. Consider supporting our press by purchasing anthologies, donating through our website (via PayPal), or placing orders for multiple copies directly through us rather than a major book distributor.

Katrina Crespin
Albuquerque, NM 2018

Contents

MEET
THE
PARADE

How to write a poem

Kevin Barger

Go to a café
Or a restaurant with a patio
Anywhere with a good amount of foot traffic
Order a coffee
Black
This is important
Order a coffee black
And don't add cream
Or sugar
Don't get any sort of mocha frappe whatever
Order a coffee black
And sit outside
Hopefully it isn't raining
In an ideal world you will be wearing a black turtleneck
and a beret
But this isn't required
What is required is coffee
Black
You sitting outside
And a good amount of foot traffic

Open your notebook in front of you
Hold on to your pen and don't set it down
Take a sip of your coffee
Let the bitterness overwhelm your tongue
And watch the people on the sidewalk walk by
Wait
Watch the people on the sidewalk walk by
And wait

Take another sip of coffee
Let the bitterness overwhelm your tongue
And wait

Find the most attractive person walking by
This is the most important
Wait to find the most attractive person walking by
And then get creepy

Do not take your eyes off of this person
Not for a moment
Don't glance away if they see you looking
Don't pretend that you're looking somewhere else
Stare at the most attractive person walking by
Place your pen to paper and examine them

Start with their hair
(Unless you're into balding men
Then start with their scalp
But I assume you're not so start with their hair)
Write about its texture
Its color
Imagine it gliding over your fingers
Over your skin
The way it would feel brushing against your neck
What does it smell like?
How does it taste?

Move down to their eyes
Look through them
Explain how the world looks to them
How you would want to look to them
Imagine them crying

Taste their tears
Imagine them laughing
And the light glistening off their irises
Write it down

Move down to their lips
Feel their lips pressed against yours
Take a sip of coffee
Fall in love with this person
Taste their breath
Their tongue
Feel them nibble on your earlobe
And whisper their secrets

Write their secrets
Write about the goosebumps they leave on your flesh
Write about the curve of their neck
Their breath pushing their clavicle
Forward
And down
Forward
And down
Move down their shoulders
Their arms embracing you
Your hands on their hips

Write about their hips
The sway of their hips
Their legs entwined in yours
Write about the first time you will make love
The sound of their voice as they whisper your name
The passionate calling beside candlelight

If you're not currently single
This isn't cheating
It's art
You're a poet
And this poem is demanding you
To write about having sex
With the most attractive person walking by
So write it without guilt
Without remorse
As you feel their touch on your ribcage
The lump they create in your throat
The salt they leave on your lips
Write it

Write it
And then take a sip of coffee
Look down at what you've written
Read everything that you've written
Notice it's not enough
And look back up
To see that they're gone

Kevin Barger

Kevin Barger has been a Swimming with Elephants Publications author since 2015 when his collection, *Observable Acts (ISBN-13: 978-0692404553)*, was chosen for publication through the 2014 Open Call for chapbooks. You can find it at all major book outlets including Amazon, Barnes and Nobel, and Powell's Books.

Kevin Barger is a performance poet and writer based in Asheville, NC. His first book, *Observable Acts*, reached #12 on Amazon's Best Gay & Lesbian Poetry Best Sellers list. He has performed in many festivals and events including the Lake Eden Arts Festival, the Lexington Avenue Arts and Fun Festival, Individual World Poetry Slam, and Southern Fried. He has also appeared at both the Asheville Fringe Festival and Capitol Fringe as a member of the Poetry Cabaret. When not writing or performing you can find him hiking the Appalachians, cooking a delicious meal, goofing off in a kayak, or playing with clay and calling it pottery.

the magazine

Bassam

when the women at the office
ask what's the secret to my weight loss,
i do not want to tell them

i remain silent,
because any reply
sounds too much like
the growling of a stomach
that skipped breakfast and lunch,
tastes like endless
cheesecake and chocolate chip cookies,
baked falsities sprinkled with
the confectionary powder
i would much rather
snort than eat

i want to tell them that
i'm aiming for my birth weight,
how my mother named her
7-pound-8-ounce baby after
the Arabic word for smile,
and yet each laughing child
i ever held inside was interred beneath
discarded nourishment given life from
the mouth she worked hard to feed,
until she couldn't keep up,
poverty-struck with the backhand
a father that knocked the
child support out of her

while living a lavish life of gluttony,
watching the flesh of his
flesh starve like dessert vulture
circling pray waiting to lay blame

i want to tell them about the
all-you-can-eat buffet of my nightmares,
where parts of my lukewarm life lay
latently underprepared over hot ground,
waiting to be picked up, processed,
bludgeoned, bloody, bones
so rare you can still hear the cries
from the abattoir,
piercing meat behind my throat
with finger-sharp weapons
decapitating myself with every
fat joke i choke on,
each flush like a cursed nursery cry,
as i lay in bathroom baptismal

there's something Freudian
to be said about fulfilling
the development of the ego,
but there is no growth:
the only shrink i desire
is shame and pain,
sadistically sardonic sorrow
that i was never meant to be satiated,
only to fit in, between
playground pavement cracks,
hiding in stalls and fighting
catholic school fugue in
confessional booth refuge,

bullies and sanctimony
from teachers unbelieving
of their crimes or my testimony,
to come home from prison
every day to cupboards
full of survival,
snacks and abjection
to remedy their rejection

forgive me heavenly mother
for i have sinned; i ate

i canonize myself to pay penance
with diet pill rosaries reciting
hail mary,
starved of grace,
only blessed being as woman,
pray for me now, that mine is
last supper at the hour of my death,
in Eucharist hunger,
if i could just sin,
just one more meal,
one more bite,
one more prayer,
one more pallbearer to my misery
atop a six-foot deep toilet
that isn't building a body
but burying one

i reply to the women at the office
with a lie:
"diet and exercise!"
I should have said

"dying and exorcism,"
realizing that trigger warnings are useless
in a world of bullet casings
that would starve itself empty
just to look like
the inside of a magazine.

Bassam

Bassam was first published with Swimming with Elephants Publications in early 2018 after the 2017 Open Call for chapbooks. Their collection, *bliss in die/unbinging the underglow (ISBN-13: 978-0999892992)*, is available at most major bookstores including Barnes and Nobel, Amazon, and Powell's City of Books.

Bassam (they/them or xe/xim) is a spoken word poet, proud auntie, and settler residing on the traditional territory of the Dish with One Spoon Wampum Belt Covenant (Anishinaabe, Haudenosaunee, Huron-Wendatt, and Mississaugas of the New Credit). they are a member of the League of Canadian Poets, an executive board member with Spoken Word Canada, and has toured Turtle Island performing spoken word. Bassam earned title of national poetry slam champion at the Canadian Festival of Spoken Word (CFSW) in 2016 with the Guelph Poetry Slam team, and Canadian Individual Poetry Slam (CIPS) finalist in 2017. they were editor-in-chief for 'these pills don't come in my skin tone,' a poetry collection exclusively by Black, Indigenous, and People of Colour (BIPOC) on the topic of mental health and illness, released in fall 2017.

The Problem with You and Me

Emily Bjustrom

The problem began with me,
snot- crying, tangled in my curls
locked away in my room.

The locked door moved through me and became me
and I am gutted.

> Now I lean into the future like a drunk.
> Take me home, I say.

The problem began with you too
deep in a book
about Love
with a capital L and the tragedies inside it.

And so you read until you became the book,
a tragedy breathing.

Look at you,
A white sail on cruel seas,
handsome and cavalier,

and me, crude but pretty,
rough in my pale skin.

> Take me home, I say.

Emily Bjustrom

Emily Bjustrom is a public school teacher. She lives in Albuquerque, New Mexico and loves to write about the desert landscape and her life inside it.

Emily Bjustrom was first published with Swimming with Elephants Publications in 2014 after the 2013 Open Call for chapbooks. Her chapbook, *Loved Always Tomorrow (ISBN-13: 978-0615991658)*, is available at most major bookstores including Barnes and Nobel, Amazon, and Powell's City of Books.

Crossroads

Matthew Brown

I don't know if it's the Burqeño in me,
but I have always felt more at home
in The Warzone than Rio Rancho.

Respect - for the steady drudge
of stolen shopping carts down
Zuni and San Mateo.

To the Dollar Tree pilgrim
and thrift store aficionado,
bounty hunter of the Goodwill,
and first-of-the-month
food pantry regulars.

I got you.

I ain't afraid to hold your hand,
ask for your name, in decency.

We ain't in no rush, either.

For those of us too fast in the head,
I know a house down Alvarado
with enough tar to bring you
slow motion somber respite,
the kind nod-you-good
molasses heavy high
that leaves even the cynic
a dew eyed n' dreary

sidewalk navel gazer.

And for those dull days,
I know a dead drop behind the 7/11
with more crank
than you can shake a piston at
just don't go reaching for things
that don't belong to you
without paying
what you owe.

People here do get shot,
just not for the reasons
you think.

If you're on a schedule
but not a budget,

there's a methadone clinic
down the street
that will dose you up,
send you on your way.
No questions asked.
No time for pleasantries,
No shirt.
No shoes.
No te preocupes.
revolving door-open policy,
all patrons welcome.

There isn't room to discriminate
when there isn't room at all.

Me, I work the prevention clinic
down the way and across the station.
You won't ever see me unless you need to
-pray you never need to
but I got you then,
same as now.

If you lend me your hand
I will read the crimson of your blood.
Weigh out our options.
Bleed through the shame.

We don't know
what we don't know,
but what we can't cure,
we can manage.

That's what we do.
We manage.

Sunup to sunset
we push carts and IV's
through veins and crowded streets.

Damage control.
Prevention.

Empty childhood.
Full stomach.

The Mayor and all them comfortables
call this the "International District"
but if you ain't from the block

you're a tourist, same as me.

I get to leave the warzone

but there's something here
that won't leave me.

At the corner of Big Lots
and 7/11 is the most honest
intersection in Albuquerque:

a crossroads where
poverty and addiction
and white catholic God
find each other
amidst the glass
and tar of the streets.

Matthew Brown

Matthew Brown's chapbook, *Verbrennen (ISBN-13: 978-0615954684),* was published in late 2014 after being chosen from the 2013 Open Call for chapbooks. It is available at most major bookstores including Barnes and Nobel, Amazon, and Powell's City of Books.

Matthew Brown is a queer Afro-Latino writer and spoken word artist from Albuquerque, New Mexico. Matthew's writing is an open soapbox that questions faith, war, suicide. love, and forgiveness. He currently studies Psychology and Political Science at the University of New Mexico.

Matthew is well recognized performance poet, a 2013 Brave New Voices finalist, three time Southwest Shootout Champion, and the 2015 Albuquerque Grand Slam Champion.

Pixie Cut

Courtney A. Butler

My pixie cut is
one part magic
one part fuck-you-up

Deconstruction
Confronting my face every day
with no room for flounce

Androgynous/femme with intention
Giving you nothing in return
A gauntlet
with no place for your parade
A mirror
where cracked masculinity crumbles

Ground zero
to recharge batteries of bodily autonomy
I come here post-death
Post-heartbreak
Post-rape

There is no cut sharper than
"You'd be so much prettier with longer hair!"
As if pretty was the point
As if beautiful was a place to live and pay taxes
As if attracting you is the end of my every journey-
barefoot, alive, feral

No concern of mine

your sexuality shrinks
with the length of my locks

I was not made to be consumed

My pixie cut is my hiding place
My tree house
I'm hanging upside-down
Stripping off my mama's pantyhose
after a night at the ballet

Hoarding red lipstick
Painting my face with war symbols, practicing my aim

My pixie cut is
when my hair is not a handle to grab and bow my back

My solace

A homecoming

and just before you decide
you understand my resurrections-
I will grow my hair
snake it around your neck
and hang you

Courtney A. Butler

Courtney A. Butler's collection, *Wild Horses (ISBN-13: 978-0998462356),* was published in late 2017 after winning third place in a SwEP's 2017 chapbook competition. Her collection is available at most major bookstores including Barnes and Nobel, Amazon, and Powell's City of Books.

Courtney Alyssa Butler grew up in south Texas, which accounts for her very decisive twang when she's been drinking just a little too much, or supremely pissed off. She attended St. Andrew's University in North Carolina, mostly because it had ponies and green grass to play in, but ended up with a double major nonetheless. Now, she works in the non-profit sector by day, while doing hair, special effects makeup, and writing at night…like Batman but with more flair. You can find her first book of poetry, *Season for Season,* at St. Andrew's University Press, Laurinburg, NC. If you're interested in poetry-in-progress, or the rambles of a mad woman, you can also check out her blogs:

TheCourtRose at thecourtrose.blogspot.com
and
Un Bel Mondo at thecourtrose-
abeautifulworld.blogspot.com

Talking to My Mother about Suicide and #MeToo, 2018

SaraEve Fermin

She said a hundred times. She said a thousand times
.- Dave Matthews Band

I'm not saying I'm sure I know what happened. What I know is this- if it happened to someone else and I didn't warn them, I don't know how I would sleep at night. I mean, until the medication, I didn't sleep. What I know is this- I'm not the only one who has been harassed/ violated/ manipulated/ gaslighted/ date raped/ assaulted, but I am the one people keep asking about. I mean, no one ever asked me, outright, what happened, how I became this Pandora's Box of secret violations, names redacted from the reports. Why my name is the only one they want in blood. What I know is this- when my mother asked me about the #MeToo movement, I told her I was one of them. I mean, I defended my right to stay silent for so long. Even to my own family, I defended myself. Even when I needed to untangle what was what and who stood where in the end, instead I defended my decision to stay silent. To keep the names and details to myself. What I know is this- sometimes, I dream about him and fear waking up with his name in my mouth. I mean, I have dreams where I am simply a rabbit caught in the wolf pen. The last thing I remember before waking up is the taste of blood. What I know is this- I know enough to stay away. I mean, I still don't feel like I am doing enough. He is still out there; no one is holding him accountable. They want our blood instead.

SaraEve Fermin

SaraEve Fermin's collection, *You Must Be This Tall to Ride* (ISBN-13: 978-0692735350), was published in the summer of 2016 by Swimming with Elephants Publications, LLC. Her collection is available at most major bookstores including Barnes and Nobel, Amazon, and Powell's City of Books.

SaraEve is a performance poet and epilepsy advocate from northeast New Jersey. A 2015 Best of the Net nominee, she has performed for both local and national events, including the 2013 Women of the World Poetry Slam, the Epilepsy Foundation of Greater Los Angeles 2015 Care and Cure Benefit to End Epilepsy in Children and as a reader for Great Weather for MEDIA at the 2016 NYC Poetry Festival on Governors Island. You might have met her volunteering at various national poetry slams. A Contributing Editor for *Words Dance Magazine* and Book Reviewer at *Swimming with Elephants Publications,* her work can be found or in *GERM Magazine, Yellow Chair Review, Drunk in a Midnight Choir* and the University of Hell Press anthology *We Can Make Your Life Better: A Guidebook to Modern Living, among others.* She believes in the power of foxes and self-publishing.

Learn more:
http://saraeve41.wix.com/saraevepoet
Instagram: SaraEve41

The softest wings

Wil Gibson

There is no way for me to be
uncomfortable for someone
without showing it.

Myself,

I change

position
            in my seat,

        or

Step
   on
     my
       own
           feet.

A small way to cope
with my   discomfort for others

is to make   myself
physically
              uncomfortable.

I know that this
      does not help them,
does not make   them feel better.

My lack of physical comfort
makes me more comfortable.

Movement is my comfort,
I suffer   from an
unease at rest,
          find odd comfort in the
quiet afforded by

physical
                    white noise.

This silence is not awkward;
feels

honest,
as

the moment
just after
a car crash,

or

the   after
someone has   begun
to die, and   also   after;
                    the strange beautiful tinge
of blue that their   skin turns when
they stop
being   able
    to

25

breathe;

the instant a

newborn deer
walks,

or an ugly butterfly
unfurls
itself. Those

soft, awkward, and
most authentic wings.

Wil Gibson

Wil Gibson has two full length poetry books published through Swimming with Elephants Publications, LLC: *Quitting smoking, falling in and out of love, and other thoughts about death. (ISBN-13: 978-0692670439)* published in 2016, and *Unease at Rest (ISBN-13: 978-0999892954)* in 2018. His books are available at all major book stores.

Wil Gibson is a writer that currently lives in Humboldt County, California where the trees are big. He has had several collections published by kind people, and has been included in a number of anthologies and lit mags both online and in print. He has travelled across the country reading poems anywhere folks let him, has been on seven National Poetry Slam teams from coast to coast, and would like to pet your dog and give you a hug, if you don't mind.

Find more info at wilgibson.com

Burque Summer Solstice

Manuel Gonzalez

Summertime heat creates
mirages off the asphalt
playing tricks on our eyes.
Burque and her secrets
are whispered on the wind
when we listen.

Paletas and sticky smiles
on the faces of *mocosos*
running free without a care in the heat.

The elders know where to find escape
from the hot Zia sun.

The river finds her
home in the Bosque
where we can find solace
solitude
and silence
in the middle of a bustling
metropolis.

Burque,
where the thirst of
the *tierra*
is quenched by a late afternoon
monsoon
sun shining through the raindrops
like diamonds.

Precious gems of our memories,
the smell of rain
flashbacks of puddle jumping.

We celebrate the rain in the desert
like a long lost friend
returning home.
The streets shine
new and clean
after the flood recedes,
but our parents still
tell the children of
La Llorona
to keep us safe
and away from the deadly ditches.

Arroyos and *acequias* that carry
our dream to irrigate
the *milpas* in the South Valley,
growing the same
corn beans and squash.
The three sisters
that were introduced to our ancestors
long ago.
The *acequias*
carry dreams to quench the thirst,
and feed us until our *panza llena*
and our *corazon es contento.*

White dragonflies dance
in the amber light of
sunset.
Burque,

so full of history
and culture,
inviting,
welcoming,
with pride,

Orgullo.

As our skies,
as big as our imaginations,
hold clouds like floating cathedrals
or carry hot air balloons
on a crisp morning.
Listening to KABQ
while we clean house,
two stepping with a broom
to Tiny Morrie, Al Hurricane,
or Manny and the Casanovas,
New Mexico Music!

Born and bred
like *calabacitas*
with corn and green chile
or homemade tortillas.
Albuquerque,
where we honor traditions and history,
sage smoke,
and Chimayo red chile.

Fishing at Tingley Beach
early in the morning
before the ducks wake up.
Burque is who we were.

It's who we are.
It's the legacy we pass on to our children,
like cruising Central,
old Route 66,
on a Sunday afternoon
in a 1963 Chevy,
original and clean,
playing oldies.
Those oldies that remind us of how far we've come.
Cruising all the way to South Valley Gardens,
growing community
under our Zia sun
blazing in the sky.

We celebrate each other's
food
music
dance
drum beat
heart beat
sacred blessing from the creator.

We are flamenco
and Danza Azteca,
jingle dress
and two step,
breakdance
and rancheras.
Our heartbeat is the rhythm
we live our lives to.

Our connection
to this land,

31

this mountain,
this sky!
Our collective sweat,
and tears in our eyes.
Memories we share
of river water
and cottonwood trees,
a symphony of *chicharras,*
that hypnotizing drone
is the late summer song
that our day dreams dance to.
In harmony we hear the crickets
take over the night.

Our singing
with *gritos* that cry out to the sky!
When the sun sets behind the west mesa
and the Sandias ripen
for the brief fleeting moment
before it gets dark,
our pink mountains majesty
holds us in her arms.
Another night in the Duke City
and *jitos* and *jitas*
are safe and sleeping.
The *viejitas*'s say their prayers
and light their candles,
and another Albuquerque summer is laid to rest
to become memories and stories.
The stories we share
as Burquenos.

Manuel Gonzalez

City of Albuquerque Poet Laureate Emeritus (2016-2018) Manuel González, is a performance poet who began his career in the poetry slam.

Manuel has represented Albuquerque on a national level as a member of the Albuquerque poetry slam team 2000, 2002, 2003, 2007. He has appeared on the PBS show, ¡COLORES!: My word is my power and again on ¡COLORES! 9/23/2017. Manuel also has a collection of his poetry published by Swimming with Elephants Publications, LLC entitled, ...*but my friends call me Burque (ISBN-13: 978-0692281512)* published in 2014.

Manuel teaches workshops on self-expression through poetry in high schools and youth detention centers. He also facilitates art therapy programs to help at risk and incarcerated youth find an outlet through art.

Opuntia

Sarita Sol Gonzalez

It is dark
but the shine of the moon
dusts the desert
in a gentle glow.
In this dim caress of light
cacti become hypnotic shades of
blues, greens, and maroons.
Colors never seen
in the brightness of the day.
As life floats
in to a subconscious state,
an hourglass flying in the distance
reminds us of time passing by.
Cacti paddles search for the faintest of light
in the darkest of shadows,
just like the rest of us.
As the world awakens from its slumber
the cacti return to its stone flower state
basking in the rays of light from the sweet sunrise.
We hunger
for its spiny, succulent, magenta fruit
and fleshy green nopales.
The sun chases away the colors of the night.
Life again pauses
in the heat of the desert,
but the cacti remain.
It is built for these hardships,
so are we.

Sarita Sol Gonzalez

Sarita Sol González is a 13 year old performance poet from Albuquerque, New Mexico. Sarita has been published in various poetry anthologies from Swimming With Elephants Publications, has self-published a chapbook, and in 2016 published *Burquenita* (Swimming With Elephants Publications, 2016).

Sarita was a featured speaker at Albuquerque TEDxYouth 2015. In April of 2016, Sarita had the honor of being asked by the then US Poet Laureate Juan Felipe Herrera, to perform with him at the Library of Congress in Washington DC. Sarita was awarded the AHCC 2016 President's Award for her accomplishments in poetry by the president of the AHCC.

Sarita's love for her familia and her community reflect in her writing.

Wounds

Katrina K Guarascio

I don't want
to forget you.

But I know
space creates distance,
creates forgetfulness,
changes the tone
of our voices
till they are no longer
recognizable.

I could carry
the photograph
of you wearing
flannel and frown
looking after me
as I drove away
for only so long
before it frays
and distorts.

The memory
of the strength of your arms,
the kindness in your touch,
the colors of your eyes
offering secrets and comforts,
the way I hung on your lip
and sunk into your skin
all the reasons I told you

36

       I would always love you,
slips from heart and mind.

I wish I still had
that slash in my heart
baring your name.
The one time healed.
The one forgetfulness
is taking from me.

Not all wounds
are asked to mend.
Some I would like to keep,
run my fingers
over scar tissue,
and smile
in sweet reminiscence
of a man who
once gave me
a world.

Katrina K Guarascio

Katrina K Guarascio has three publications with Swimming with Elephants Publications, LLC: *September (ISBN-13: 978-1494712693)*, *the fall of a sparrow (ISBN-13: 978-0692220153),* and *my verse (ISBN-13: 978-0615957111).* All available though most major booksellers.

A writer and teacher living in Albuquerque, NM, Katrina remains an active member of the local poetry community. She has worked as an editor for various literary magazines and small presses, along with hosting poetry workshops and producing various poetry performances. Along with many small press and e-zine publications, she is the author of two chapbooks of poetry, *Hazy Expressions* and *More Fire than Sun*, and two out of print full-length poetry collections, *A Scattering of Imperfections* and *They Don't Make Memories Like That Anymore.*

Although her work has taken her into the realm of publishing and fiction, she continues to publish her poetry under her maiden name and keep a separation between her poetry and publishing endeavors.

the bones of this land

Kat Heatherington

i grew up on a mining claim
in the mountains of central arizona.
bear with me.
i grew up in a nice-enough house
on the poor side of a small town
in the mountains of central arizona.
i walked to school every day,
got a job in a thrift store when i turned 15,
and spent every second weekend
and then some
up at the mine with my dad.

this was not a hobby.
my dad drank hard.
the desert dried him out,
more or less. saved his life.
like a cactus, he retained
what he most valued.
books, beer, his daughters.
the desert gave back clarity,
integrity. silence.
his skin baked brown under that long sun.

the old copper mine had played out
decades ago, the top collapsed
into an open pit. an ore mill straddled
the hillside above. junk abounded.
old cars, oil barrels, you name it.
the product and refuse of industry.

dad's buddy Chris would come
up to the claim with beer money
and they stood there talking
in the shade of one real big oak,
where dad kept his camper parked
near the edge of the bluff,
how they were gonna get that mill running,
and make a million bucks.
or even a living.
they didn't try very hard.
it was enough
to stand in that shade, that sun,
and take in each day. the sun
and the solitude filled him up.
i spent my nights by the light of a kerosene heater,
in the old stone cabin, its shelves
piled with antique chemistry in jars,
enticing and dangerous.
my sister collected interesting rocks,
set them up in a pile by the old mine tailings.
we read books, talked with dad,
sat in the shade, or explored scrub-covered hillsides,
and the seep down the hill,
at the old cave-mine entrance,
where a cottonwood grew, and watercress,
while dad sipped his beer, read, smoked cigarettes,
year after year. we ate lentils cooked with an onion,
circus animal cookies, orange crush. it sounds
like poverty, and it was, but those were good years.
twenty years after leaving that place, my sister and i
went back to scatter his ashes. it was not
the place he died, or the place he'd lived the longest.
but it was the only place that made sense.

we had the idea that we'd stand
on the edge of that bluff, under the old oak
that sheltered those years, and throw ash to the wind.

we found the mine. the road was gone,
locked and rucked into hillocks and destroyed.
we walked up.
the old mill was gone. how do you erase
something the size of an ore mill?
a wide flat spot remained, buzzing with
bees drinking nectar from horehound and mallow.
not a single gear or barrel or oil stain remained.
i found one steel washer in the dirt, and a piece of plastic
–
a relief. this tiny human thing.
we walked on.
the bluff was gone. the old oak, vanished.
the land just – stopped.
a tree big enough to live under.
a hillside wide enough to grow up on.
washed down the gully. we felt
that we had imagined our childhoods.

the bones of the land
spoke to my bones.
the horizon remained,
limitless, green, unspeaking.
pinned under the vast blue
of that desert sky, and, always,
offering up to it.
nothing had changed, except us.
everything had changed, except us.

we ate lunch surrounded by manzanita and silence.
i found one stone, a pebble,
flecked with mortar
from the vanished cabin beneath the oaks.
i took it home.
now, even that trace is gone.

we scattered his ashes off the new edge of the bluff.
scrub oak and manzanita accepted
the dust of our father's body,
as they had accepted the dust of his life.
i piled the last handful of ash
beside a tiny purple wildflower.
as we watched, an ant walked on it,
took a fleck of bone carefully in its mandibles,
and walked away.
now even that trace is gone.
it lives, like him,
only in our bones.

Kat Heatherington

Kat Heatherington's collection, *the bones of this land (ISBN-13: 978-0998462363),* was published in 2017 after winning first place in a SwEP's 2017 chapbook competition. The collection is available at most major bookstores including Barnes and Nobel, Amazon, and Powell's City of Books.

Kat Heatherington is a queer ecofeminist poet, sometime artist, pagan, and organic gardener. She has been living in Albuquerque since 1998, when she moved here to earn a Master's in English at UNM.

In 2007 she collaborated with a group of three other unrelated adults to buy land in the Rio Grande Valley and form Sunflower River intentional community, sunflowerriver.org. Ten years and many life lessons later, Sunflower River is still going strong, and still providing plenty of material to write poems about.

Kat's work primarily addresses the interstices of human relationships and the natural world. She has several self-published chapbooks, available from the author at yarrow@sunflowerriver.org. Her work can be read at https://sometimesaparticle.org.

Where There Were Waves

Brian Hendrickson

Night is not your first choice,
When you would be born into dream
A scattering of baitfish.

All day your words assembled one another
Into the usual predators;
Shadows of unknown intentions;

Anemones lurching
Up from shipwreck.
Now, in the settled dark,

Watch as words gather
Over the open sea of your aloneness
Like distant clouds lit by their own silent lightning.

The tide withdrawn, you walk where
Hours ago there were waves.
All around you, periwinkles tunneling.

Even the condominiums
With their disastrous walls of stars
Can never own you here.

Something deeper than you know
Is dragging at your bones
Like a current in the sand.

Somehow, you must learn
To carry what you can
Back into the turbulent schools of dawn.

Brian Hendrickson

Brian Hendrickson's collection of poetry, entitled *Of Children / And Other Poor Swimmers (ISBN-13: 978-0692256350),* was published by Swimming with Elephants Publications, LLC in September 2014 after winning second place in our yearly chapbook competition. His collection is available at most major bookstores including Barnes and Nobel, Amazon, and Powells City of Books.

Brian Hendrickson's poems have appeared or are forthcoming in a range of publications, including *Indiana Review, North Carolina Literary Review,* and *New York Quarterly.*

For his poetry Brian has been nominated for a 2011 Pushcart Prize and Best of the Net award, recognized as a 2013 finalist for Smartish Pace's Erskine J. Poetry Prize, and awarded a 2013 New Mexico-Arizona Book Award for appearing in Beatlick Press' *La Llorona* anthology.

Since earning an MFA in Creative Writing and Literary Arts from the University of Alaska Anchorage, Brian has taught and tutored writing at colleges and correctional facilities in Alaska, Florida, North Carolina, and New Mexico.

How We Were

Zachary Kluckman

The lovers never touch.
The first thing I notice,
each holds their keys easily;
as if comfortable with leaving,
as is

the car's already running.

Conversation only
a prelude to parting.

Her body is the color of tongues,
reminds me how one never wets
their lips for the goodbye kiss,
as if rough is how we wrestle
with alone,
how we show our true face
for the first time,
as if goodbye
is the first permission we give
ourselves to be naked
in front of others.

Zachary Kluckman

Zachary Kluckman's, *Some of It is Muscle* *(ISBN-13: 978-1494387778),* was published by Swimming with Elephants Publications in December 2013, making it the second collection released from SwEP.

A performance poet since 2006, Zachary Kluckman has been writing poetry for 25 years. A Pushcart Prize nominee and recipient of the Red Mountain Press Poetry Prize, his work appears in print globally in such publications as the New York Quarterly and Cutthroat, as well as numerous anthologies. Featured on over 500 radio stations, with appearances on many of the nation's most notorious stages, he is an accomplished spoken word artist. He serves as the Spoken Word Editor of the Pedestal. Twice recognized for making world history, he is the creator of the Slam Poet Laureate Program and an organizer for the 100 Thousand Poets for Change program, the largest poetry reading in history.

His first collection of poems, *Animals In Our Flesh*, was published in 2012 by Red Mountain Press. He has a collection titled, *The Curious Circus*, from Uncola Press. An activist and youth advocate, he lives in New Mexico with his four children.

Not Today, Today

Paulie Lipman

Some days, you live
Others, you survive
and some you just
exist

While you are doing
any of these, the other two
will try to convince you
that you ain't shit

I do not own the
perfect font or stock photo
to properly express my current overload
I have no two sentence meme
to sum up the fact that
my brain chemistry
will not allow me to
fully human today

Today
I am not mystical,
in awe of the
universe's majesty,
or made of stardust
I am simply a
water/meat vehicle
with an aspirated
computer engine, sputtering
the same command line:

Continue
Continue
Continue

Today
I shared 3 minutes
of silence and tail wag
with a dog, and in that
no judgement
no complex sentences
no inspirational quotes
just mutual understanding
and as much smile
as a dog/I could muster

Some would
call this Simplicity
Some might
label it Zen
I am not a Buddhist
but have studied the
meaning of both those words and
the balance between Being/Nothingness
to know that to name that moment
would be completely
missing the point

Today I was told
don't be a wallflower
to Life's astonishing dance
but today the
lights are too bright
the music, so loud

steps, too brash
the strobe
shadowplays every trauma
that's tried to murder me
flicker kicks my fists
whirlwinds my boots to
anger/dervish/spin kick
the sincerest of waltzes
whipped into a mosh pit
where the only beauty found
will be the blood

Not today
Today, I am
one step removed
and mute
Today I will
observe and
exist and survive

Tomorrow,
tomorrow we'll see
about living

Paulie Lipman

Paulie Lipman's chapbook, *from below/denied the light (ISBN-13: 978-0998462325)*, was published in January of 2018. Lipman's chapbook was the first collaboration between Sugar Booking Entertainment and Swimming with Elephants Publications.

Paulie Lipman is a former bartender/ bouncer/ record store employee/ Renaissance Fair worker/ two time National Poetry Slam finalist and a current loud Jewish/Queer/ poet/writer/performer. His work has appeared in the anthology *'We Will Be Shelter'* (Write Bloody Publishing) as well as *The Emerson Review, Drunk in a Midnight Choir, Voicemail Poems, pressure gauge*, and *Prisma* (Zeitblatt Fur Text & Sprache).

I Have Many Names/ Tengo Muchos Nombres

Jessica Helen Lopez

YOU may call me Malinche, goddess of grass
Indi-gena woman
of the kidnapped clan

Rosetta-Stone tongue
glassy rain-soaked Imperial jade,

Moctezuma's posioned
trade with the white-skinned transgressor,

Quet-zal-coat
-cloaked Cortes

Flesh over the forged heat of Spanish blade, the dutch,
the french

The mulatto/the mestiza/Africana
raped daughters of the Doctrine
of Discovery

You may call me the descendent
of the deceased.

The disappeared. The Pillaged. The
Blood-quantum, kick-back treaty fed by the belly-fat of
land grant lies.

I have many names,
thousands years' old names.

Ancient, mighty names.
but today you may call me
seven generations missing from my grandmother.

Tonatzin. Malinalli. Tlatzoteotl. Ometeol.

I am the blood-lineage, sacrificial ancestor

progeny of the gone-missing women

call me *Maquiladora* – flower of the factories
Woman of Juarez
twice-bit and betrayed both
by my own kin and the foreign rapist

You may call me rage.
Riteous.
Vengeful.

Tengo muchos nombres

You may call me *soldadera*, matriarch of the Mexican
Revolution.
I was never anyone's lover.
No Pancho Villa bed-warmer.
Bullets and braids, hands thick like the skin of tamal
This is what *you* may call me.
No yo soy Joaquin.

You may call me *Llorrona*, shape-shifter, picket-line
provacateur
brown beret, skin-walker
woman of the field,

hands of callus,
picker of *fresa, chile, cebolla* and the grape on the vine
We the legions of farmworkers bent at the spine,
Fingers deep into the dark earth

Today they will call me wet-nurse,
wet-back, under-the-table paid
brown nanny
Breast-milk by proxy

But I birth me
In the shape of me

blade-sharp
obsidian, flint and fired stone
I am the blood-letting and the baptismal

I have many names
Tengo
Muchos
Muchos
Nombres

But *you* may invoke me brown-skinned *Puta*
Xola Xingona,
Spelled with an X like the Mexica do

My ancestors who run wild in my blood,
My mixed, messy, colonized AND triumphant blood

You may call me double-tongued and code-switcher,
River crosser, water diviner

Border dweller and burnt sage
You know me as #metoo
the bridged hair of Frida's brow
Snapped spinal column survivor

The late night mariachi howl, eater of filth

You may call me *Pocha, Jota, Bruja* and lit-from-within
My name an anglicized
stain

a de-loused campesino
short hair and clipped tongue
somewhere in the middle of Indio
California – fruit basket of the world

But *now*
you may invoke me
Dolores, Lorna, Sandra, Maria,
Josefina, Gloria, Diana the Huntress
Emma Gonzalez AND Alicia Garza

Patrisse,
Opal,
Audre
Lorde writer and patron saint who watches over us all

You may call me
La Cazadora
Huntress
No regrets

I am the Keeper of the Dead

Tengo muchos nombres
You may call me Thought Woman, carrier of stories
jeweled egg of a diaphonous web
My children spring forth from me, silver-headed
Spindle-soft, ready to re-create the world
Seventh generation rising

I am *un mal flora*,
The bad flower who grew despite
Your attempt
to re-name that
which is nameless.

Jessica Helen Lopez

Jessica Helen Lopez's chapbook, *cunt.bomb.* *(ISBN-13: 978-1494451165)*, was the first book published by Swimming with Elephants Publications in December of 2013. Her follow up collection, *The Language of Bleeding (ISBN-13: 978-0692362150),* was published with SwEP in preparation for her travels to Nicaragua.

Jessica Helen Lopez was named the City of Albuquerque Poet Laureate from 2014-2016. She has been a featured writer for 30 Poets in their 30's by MUZZLE magazine. Lopez is a nationally recognized award-winning slam poet, and holds the title of 2012 and 2014 Women of the World (WOW) City of ABQ Champion.

Her first collection of poetry, *Always Messing With Them Boys* (West End Press, 2011) made the Southwest Book of the Year reading list and was also awarded the Zia Book Award presented by NM Women Press. Her publication, *Cunt.Bomb.* (Swimming with Elephants Publications 2014), is a chapbook collection of poems focusing on the powers of the feminine. She is the founder of La Palabra – The Word is a Woman collective created for and by women and gender-identified women, and a Ted Talk speaker alum.

Vulcan, Albuquerque 2009-2013

Kristian Macaron

One morning,
long before our hearts
were formed, the city awoke
to smoke on the West Mesa,
spuming spirals melting into
a florescent Albuquerque dawn.
It was not a reawakening, but
tires burning in calderas
mimicking melting basalt hearts
            that would never come unbound.

I wondered once
what it must feel like
for a heart to grow cold,
all the embers quietly dying.
The chemistry of cooling is
physics and pressure,
collision and currents,
transfer, and equilibrium.
We cannot keep a temperature;
we can fuel a fire,
but you cannot force a heart
to keep burning
            even when it holds your name.

Two hundred thousand years
after the scorching, my mother
told the story of the tires in the car,
on the way to somewhere (I only remember

the sun shine) without knowing what
heart of mine was cooling under
tired tears. Without knowing that once
I buried my name and a lover's on
Vulcan, scorched earth made mesa;
moments of declarations and
rattlesnakes warming in the sun.
Cooling is an absence, a noticeable
shudder and in some dreams:
        the rattle of a snake tail.

Two hundred thousand years
after the scorching, a child,
who knows of cold volcanoes, says
he'd like to know:
"What makes fire old?"
I don't hesitate when I tell him that
it takes such a long time,
we'd forget to count the seasons;
that the wind blows over magma
falling over land like a long, soft
sleep. I don't hesitate when I tell him,
but I can feel some
        warmth in me leaving:

A so slow   winter
        learning what it feels like
                for a heart to grow cold;

        The first moment of exodus,
cooling was a voice, then shiver, shard, crack.
It was shelling pomegranates in the
witching hours of a solstice.

To rend the sweet apart from
the bitter, scales off of fresh, new
skin that bleeds until it doesn't.

       Six of them—one after the other—
cold, round and full as worlds—
my hands dried with sweet
blood from teardrop shaped fruit,
some bursting. I went to bed with
no strength left to wash my hands.
It's all poured out in the breaking and
puddled in the kitchen, sudden
sweet smolder and

       all the embers   quietly dying.

Kristian Macaron

Kristian Ashley Macaron's chapbook, *Storm (ISBN-13: 978-0692468609),* was published by Swimming with Elephants Publications in June 2015.

Originally from Albuquerque, NM where she attended the University of New Mexico, Kristian received her MFA from Emerson College in Boston, Massachusetts and thus melded her love for the colorful Southwest with the stunning New England coast. Her other publications of fiction and poetry are published in *The Winter Tangerine Review, Philadelphia Stories, Duke City Fix: The Sunday Poem, Lightning Cake Journal, The Bellows American Review (The [BAR]), Ginosko Literary Journal, Elbow Room New Mexico, Watermelon Isotope*, and *Medusa's Laugh Press.*

She has taught scriptwriting at the Emerson College Pre-College Creative Writers' Workshop and currently teaches English at the University of New Mexico-Valencia Branch.

View Kristian's work at Kristianmacaron.com

Sunrise and a 15 Minute Yoga Practice

Gina Marselle

It's 6:45 a.m.
Son is up as the sun rises.
We take a quick trip to Starbucks,
order a medium roast coffee, toasted bagel,
and chocolate milk—
Had hoped he'd sleep next to his Dada
so I could do this on my own,
but he's five and follows his own intuition.
I make do.
Sweaters, sandals, morning bedheads.
It's September and 62 degrees.
We drive through the drive up, place our order—
head home, unbuckle.
Get son's bagel prepared—
Animal Mechanicals set up on the computer.
I methodically place my yoga mat.
Indulge in three sips of warm coffee.
Sigh. Absolutely beautiful.

It's 7:15 a.m.
Pull back the heavy dining room curtains,
revere the sun as it rises over the Sandias
spilling corner to corner.
Take a deep and cleansing breath in, exhale slowly.
Step onto my mat.
Begin. Forward fold, dangle side to side,
hear the cracking of bone
as I lengthen. Hands firm on the ground,
shoulder width apart.

Right, then left foot back into strong plank.
Hold, core is working.
Chaturanga into baby cobra.
Up to my first downward dog.
On a simple Sunday morning, not much more amazing
than a sunrise and a 15 minute yoga practice.

Gina Marselle

Gina Marselle is a New Mexico educator, poet, and photographer. She has worked with Swimming with Elephants Publications, LLC since its conception in December of 2013. Throughout the years she contributed photography to various book covers such as *Trigger Warning: Poetry Saved My Life,* and a short collection, *September*, which she created with author Katrina K Guarascio.

Her own collection of Photography and Poetry entitle *Fire of Prayer: A Collection of Poetry and Photography (ISBN-13: 978-0692360248)*, was published with Swimming with Elephants Publications, LLC in the summer of 2015. You can find her collection along with the other books for while she contributed photography at all major book outlets including Amazon, Barnes and Nobel, and Powell's Books.

The handmade heart

MJR Montoya

Long ago, the makers,
in the first hour of science,
when the swords of alchemy and song
prepared their surrender
to the scalpel,
and boats grew
unafraid of the tempests,

forged a child out of wood.

He was crafted from an oak
that once carried the body
of a Viking prince
and listened to Ptolemy
when the first books were
shelved in Alexandria.

His vessels were coiled
from a banyan tree,
the same that witnessed
the tobacco fires of Charleston
and lit the torches of the
Cherokee expulsion.

His eyes were painted with
añil and scarab tears
and his mouth was kissed
with the figs of Balkh
and the charcoal of Oldupai.

His clothes were cut from the
skins of red bison
and his buttons shaped from
the Pāua shells dropped
by the Hina queen at dawn

And his hat held two feathers
of a dinosaur bird whose name
is long past the lips of Adam.

Every part of him
was taken from the prayers
of conquered souls
or discarded by the
sadness of broken people.

The makers,
in the twilight of Magic and Dream,
who protected the alchemists and
mystics from a great purge,
breathed life into this child.

The boy was passed among the
makers over centuries,
each workshop a refuge
from the affairs of men,
an orphan among orphaned minds.

The boy witnessed the potter,
the puzzle box maker,
the weaver and the sculptor
the dancer and the jeweler.

He accompanied
the mask maker, the
tarot card painter, the muralist,
the clock maker,
the architect and dramatist.

His heart acquired words
forged of dying substances.
A simple pine block, soft and pliable,
became a rood of suffering
with each cloistered labor.

One fateful night, the last of them,
the clock maker, was taken
by the death factories
and crude men in cheap suits.
In desperation
the wooden boy stretched
out his hand to his friend.

Like his makers before him
he never stopped reaching.

I know because I am that boy.
These hands made this tapestry,
These hands died ten ages before these words became
flesh.
These hands have passed their time as flesh.
They have now become the machine of my blood.

This body, this artifact, is witness to the breaker of
machines,
an infectious thing that now restarts the clock

with these words I made by hand.

I am no longer here. But I
hope that I can dwell
in the clock of ages,
as created becomes creator,

the handmade heart is proof
that what is ancient is not past
and what is to come may have already expired.

And everywhere in these words that follow
is the fear of a coming midnight
and the broken mess that happened
as I adored the made
and the maker.

MJR Montoya

MJR Montoya's collection, *The Promethean Clock or Love Poems of a Wooden Boy (ISBN-13: 978-0998462349),* was published in late 2017 by Swimming with Elephants Publications, LLC after winning 2nd place in our 2017 chapbook competition. *The Promethean Clock or Love Poems of a Wooden Boy* is available at most major bookstores including Barnes and Nobel, Amazon, and Powell's City of Books.

Manuel (MJR) Montoya, was born and raised in Mora, New Mexico. He is a professor at the University of New Mexico. He blends studies of philosophy and literature with studies of international relations, economics and management to understand the evolution of the global political economy. He received his undergraduate degree at UNM, with graduate schooling from New York University, Oxford University, and Emory University. He is engaged in community work to support the creative economy, he is dedicated to work that eliminates child exploitation worldwide, and he is passionate about handmade craft – he has been an amateur watchmaker for 12 years. He has published poetry and short stories in various national publications.

Dover Base

Bill Nevins

He fell in Afghanistan
Sometime the day before

The Major couldn't find my house
And it was a stormy night in Albuquerque
So we talked by cell phone instead
No dress uniforms at my door

It was a clean shot
Straight through the heart

The Major was a father himself he said
I could hear his kid behind the phone

I could see my son reaching up to his dad

The Major called back
The Government could fly me, the Major said
To the Dignified Transfer
At Dover Base
I asked where that was
The Major said he thought it might be in Indianapolis
But he wasn't sure exactly where

I looked it up on Google and found
It is in Dover, Delaware

I don't know where he is
I know
He is beautiful there

Bill Nevins

Bill Nevin's collection, *Heartbreak Ridge and Other Poems (ISBN-13: 978-0692253762),* was published by Swimming with Elephants Publications in August of 2014.

Bill Nevins grew up Irish Catholic near and in New York City in the 1950's and 60's. He moved to northern New England and raised his three children, one of whom, Special Forces SFC Liam Nevins, died in combat in Afghanistan in 2013. Bill has lived in Albuquerque, New Mexico since 1996.

His poetry has been published in *Malpaís Review, Green Left Weekly, The Rag, Central Avenue, Sage Trail, Adobe Walls, Más Tequila Review, Special Forces Charitable Trust online, Maple Leaf Rag II, The Cornelian, KUMISS,* and other publications. His journalism is found in *The Guardian, Forward Motion, Z Magazine, RootsWorld, Hyper Active, Trend of Santa Fe, EcoSource, LOGOS, Thirsty Ear, ABQ ARTS, Local iQ, TM Transmission, The Celtic Connection, Irish American News, An Scuthan/Celtic Mirror* and other journals.

Bill has retired from teaching and divides his time between homes in Albuquerque and Black Lake, New Mexico, and traveling.

i need poems

Mary Oishi

these days i need poems
between my fingers
bulking my pillows
spinning off the ceiling fan

i need poems to sweet the oatmeal,
to cream the morning coffee

i need cupboards so full of poems you
couldn't squeeze in another can of soup

i need a poem to lock my door,
to start my car
i need poems to
bubble up through the storm drains
on my way to more poems,
an office full of poems
i need poems to populate my screens
to ring my phone

i need poems to jump into the headlines
in Arial Black 200 point type, push out
    all that is not poem

i need a world of poems--
a 7-billion-voice poem
speaking through 14 billion eyes

i need trillions of poems
twinkling at me across light years

i need poemspoemspoemspoems
a universe of nothing but--
just to keep the light on
just to keep my head
in a world gone madmadmad

Mary Oishi

Mary Oishi is one of the authors of *Rock Paper Scissors (ISBN-13: 978-0999892947)*, a collection of work she constructed with her daughter Aja Oishi. The collection, which ranges in theme and style, was published in 2018 by Swimming with Elephants Publications and is available through all major book distributors.

Mary Oishi has two poetic voices: one stark and simple like that of her Japanese ancestors, and one that echoes the rhythms of preachers from her upbringing by her American father's fundamentalist relatives. Both voices sing her songs of truth and social justice. She is the author of *Spirit Birds They Told Me* (2011) and is one of twelve U.S. poets in *12 Poetas: Antologia De Nuevos Poetas Estadounidenses* (2017), a project of the Mexican Ministry of Culture. Her poems have appeared in *Mas Tequila Review, Malpais Review, Harwood Anthology, Sinister Wisdom*, and other print and digital publications. Oishi is a public radio personality since 1996, mostly at KUNM-FM Albuquerque, where she hosts The Blues Show.

The Cradle

Maxine L Peseke

This body was not carved correctly for a baby

That's what I told myself when you fell from my womb
cradle dropping bloodied chunks of my uterine lining
when I turned my stomach inside, outside, inside again
(I tried to hold you in)

While my tree linings swung cradle
from thin branch to thin branch
only to crash, to fall, cradle and all;
and I tried to hold you in,
tried to carve my failing womb into a
cradle to house you

And she fell from the womb too soon
my womb, my body, unwilling to hold her in
while my mind was so desperate
to carve tree branches
into something sturdy

but my womb was made up of something brittle inside
and then tree branches snapped, then the cradle fell

And I wonder what my innards are carved from—
whole pieces of the child that was beginning to
stain my underthings
Tree branches so brittle,
this cradle might have been carved from bone
and I'd give up my ribcage just to hold you in

I'd give up my whole life just to know my
body was carved correctly
to make a cradle for the baby I miscarried

I'd become a carpenter just to cut down that tree
before it falls,
before cradle comes crashing down,
baby and all
and this was all happening inside of me, so I wonder:
weren't we carved from the same tree
wasn't my body strong enough to carve a
cradle rather than a casket

Weren't you strong enough to sleep through it all;
Baby, sleep, don't cry,
don't fall.

Maxine L Peseke

Maxine L. Peseke is a book reviewer, editor, and administrator with Swimming with Elephants Publications, LLC. She plays an intricate role in website and social media maintenance.

Her work has previously appeared in the Winter 2015 edition of *Catching Calliope*, in both the poetry and prose sections; and she has worked previously as a coordinator and host of Valencia County's first poetry slam and open mic, encouraging new and young writers to participate in the active poetry community in Albuquerque.

During her time as an active member of the ABQ slam poetry community, she qualified and placed third in the OUTSpoken Queer Poetry Slam Championship, in 2013, and again in 2014 when she tied for third place. In 2013, she was among the top 10 female poets in Albuquerque and competed to represent the city at the 2014 Women of the World Poetry Slam.

Lately, she loves on other writers and can be found in an snowy small town in Northern Ontario, where she finds poetry in the giggles of her two girls and in every falling leaf, though her neighbours know her as the lady who tells her dogs to stop barking all too frequently.

Good Drums

Beau Williams

A Palestinian musician
sings me a song then asks
if she frightens me.
Asks if her accent will unplug

the skin from my spine;
find my hand to the butt of my gun.
I don't own a gun.
She is not convinced.

I don't blame her.
I am every news story and
every rubbled hospital.
I have ten tanks in my chest.

I am the first white man
she has ever seen.
I am so sorry.
I send out search parties to find

her ears, her heart.
Her grandmother taught her
to become a saint of hidden things.
Her sisters taught her to be

encyclopedia fists and full shoulders
when the threat comes.
I cannot be a mouthpiece for a
battalion but I can pick up a drum.

I follow her lead.
We bumble, we stop,
we regroup, we blend.
Become composers in a foreign land.

If we could drown out bombs
with this craic, then the sky
could open like a music note.
If we could calm these fires

If we could kill this television
in a chorus of climax
we could be a fat thumb print
in a memory. We could be a moment's

hesitation and a second thought.
Her voice pulls the picture frames tight.
My percussion sews them to the walls.
I never ask what the words mean.

She never asks where I'm from.
We eat notes from the air.
That is every answer we need.
This song is not a roll in a flower bed.

This is a poem belted through
a stereo, this is six generations
in powerful ululation.
A gallery of painted rocks

and broken noses. This is a mosque
full of a good god's voice
in perfect rhythm
with a superfly beat.

Beau Williams

Beau Williams' full-length poetry collection, *Nail Gun and a Love Letter (ISBN-13: 978-0998462332),* was published in January of 2018. Williams' collection is the result of a collaboration between Sugar Booking Entertainment and Swimming with Elephants Publications. The collection is available at most major bookstores including Barnes and Nobel, Amazon, and Powell's City of Books.

Beau Williams is a fairly optimistic poet based out of Portland Maine. He co-runs a weekly poetry class at Sweetser Academy and facilitates workshops at high schools and colleges around the New England area. His work has been published in numerous poetry websites and journals.

Beau has performed internationally and nationally both as a solo artist and with the performance poetry collectives *Uncomfortable Laughter* and *GUYSLIKEYOU.* He was the Grand Slam Champion at Port Veritas in 2014 and was the Artist in Residence at Burren College in Ballyvaughan, Ireland in January of 2017. Beau's book, *Rumham*, is available for purchase on Amazon.com.

Wangari Muta Maathai

Liza Wolff-Francis

Before I learned to speak, I was a tree
fraying at the edges of my limbs.

I am most at home in the soil of Kenya,
determined against extinction.

The world is full of things my people
cannot reach, their bellies hunger,

their backs bent under sun, hands
cupped, a frenzy of tragic warmth.

I will plant a thousand trees, pay each
woman among us to plant a thousand

more. Each tree rooted to the earth,
solid identity, with voice demanding

schooling women never got. Each tree
strong in self, together a forest

breathing the most tender necessary
demands, raise the soft hairs on our

earlobes, play in the dirt of what might
have been. I once believed someone could

stop the pain of not knowing how to dream
or what to dream for, but the nights kept

ending the same way, dull hum, no
flowering, vapid moon, all beast.

Every year is the year we may flex
our muscles, pull us all up, our budding

seeds, our thick forest. I get the feeling that
without each other, rooted, we shrink,

our vision wrapped round our necks.
Without each other, a heart-shaped hole.

Together, we shift, pinned to this land
and all of this trickles down.

Liza Wolff-Francis

Liza Wolff-Francis's chapbook, *Language of Crossing (ISBN-13: 978-0692531754),* was published in the fall of 2015 by Swimming with Elephants Publications, LLC.

Liza Wolff-Francis is a poet and writer with an M.F.A. in Creative Writing from Goddard College. She was co-director for the 2014 Austin International Poetry Festival and a member of the 2008 Albuquerque Poetry Slam Team. She has an ekphrastic poem posted in Austin's Blanton Art Museum by El Anatsui's sculpture "Seepage" and her work has most recently appeared in *Edge, Twenty, unseenfiction.com, Border Senses,* and on various blogs. As a social worker, she has worked with Spanish speaking immigrant populations for twenty years. She wrote the play *Border Rising* from interviews with undocumented Mexican immigrants in Los Angeles. She currently lives in Albuquerque, NM.

Swimming with Elephants Publications, LLC
Poetry Collections and Chapbooks
Alphabetical by Title

...but my friends call my Burque
　　　Poetry by Manuel Gonzalez

22
　　　Poetry by Gigi Bella

A Fire of Prayer
　　　Poetry by Gina Marselle

BEKIMI I NËNËS / A Mother's Blessing
　　　Poetry by Jusuf Gërvalla (Author),
　　　Jack Hirschman (Translator),
　　　Idlir Azizaj (Translator)

Cunt. Bomb.
　　　A Chapbook by Jessica Helen Lopez

Elegy for a Star Girl
　　　Poetry by Christopher Grillo

For Those Who Outlast Their Pain
　　　Poetry by Niccolea Nance

from below/denied the light
　　　Poetry by Paulie Lipman

my verse,
>Poetry by Katrina K Guarascio
>Photography by Shawna Cory

Nail Gun and a Love Letter
>Poetry by Beau Williams

Observable Acts
>Poetry by Kevin Barger
>Cover Art by James Burbank

Of Small Children / and Other Poor Swimmers
>Poetry by Brian Hendrickson

Passion, Provocation, and Prophecy
>Interview and Poetry by Jack Hirshman and
>Justin Desmangles

Periscope Heart
>Poetry by Kai Coggin

Quitting smoking, falling in and out of love, and other thoughts about death
>Poetry by Wil Gibson

Rock Paper Scissors
>Poetry by Mary Oishi and Aja Oishi

Saltwater Under Brittle Sky
        Poetry by Lori DeSanti

September
        Poetry by Katrina K Guarascio
        Photography by Gina Marselle

Some of it is Muscle
        Poetry by Zachary Kluckman

Storm
        Poetry by Kristian Macaron
        Cover Art by Gwendolyn Prior

the bones of this land
        Poetry by Kat Heatherington
        Cover Art by Gwendolyn Prior

The Fall of a Sparrow
        Poetry by Katrina K Guarascio

The Promethean Clock
        Poetry by MJR Montoya

They Are All Me
        Poetry by Dominique Christina

To Anyone Who Has Ever Loved a Writer
        A Chapbook by Nika Ann

Unease at Rest
    Poetry by Wil Gibson

Verbrennen
    A Chapbook by Matthew Brown

Wild Horses
    Poetry by Courtney A. Butler
    Cover Art by Judy Marquez

You Must Be This Tall to Ride
    Poetry by SaraEve Fermin